LAO TSU AND TAOISM

Lao Tsu, an older contemporary of Confucius, was keeper of the imperial archives at Loyang in the province of Honan in the sixth century B.C. All his life he taught that "The Tao that can be told is not the eternal Tao"; but, according to ancient legend, as he was riding off into the desert to die—sick at heart at the ways of men—he was persuaded by a gatekeeper in northwestern China to write down his teaching for posterity.

The essence of Taoism is contained in the eighty-one chapters of the book—roughly 5,000 words—which have for 2,500 years provided one of the major underlying influences in Chinese thought and culture, emerging also in proverbs and folklore. Whereas Confucianism is concerned with day-to-day rules of conduct, Taoism is concerned with a more spiritual level of being.

PHOTOGRAPHY BY JANE ENGLISH
CALLIGRAPHY BY GIA-FU FENG

LAO TSU 道德經 TAO TE CHING

TRANSLATED BY GIA-FU FENG AND JANE ENGLISH

VINTAGE BOOKS   A DIVISION OF RANDOM HOUSE, INC., NEW YORK

VINTAGE BOOKS EDITION, MARCH 1997

25th-Anniversary edition copyright © 1997 by Jane English
Copyright © 1972 by Gia-fu Feng and Jane English

"A Modern Way of the Eternal Tao" by Rowena Pattee Kryder used by
permission of the author. Extract from unpublished autobiographical
writings by Gia-fu Feng used by permission of Carol Wilson. Essay and
calligraphy by Chungliang Al Huang used by permission of the author.
Extract from "What Constitutes a 'Necessary' Book" by Toinette Lippe
used by permission of the author.

The Library of Congress has cataloged the original Vintage edition
as follows:
Lao-tzŭ.
Tao te ching.
I. Feng, Gia-fu. tr.   II. English, Jane, tr.   III. Title.
[BL1900.L3F46   1972b]   299'.51'482   72-2338
Original ISBN 0-394-71833-X
Vintage ISBN: 0-679-77619-2

Random House Web address: http://www.randomhouse.com
Printed in the United States of America
21 20 19 18 17 16 15 14

It is somehow not surprising that a book that has stood the test of time for 2,500 years could inspire a modern edition that would endure twenty-five years. In the *Tao Te Ching*'s long history this edition is but a moment. However, in a human lifetime twenty-five years is a considerable span of time, a whole generation.

This is a celebration of a book that has sold well over half a million copies since its publication in 1972 and that also has German, Dutch, Finnish, Russian, Greek, and Portuguese editions. In 1972, Nixon had just been to China, the counter-culture of the late 1960s had increased awareness of Oriental philosophy and spiritual practices, and the environmental movement was beginning to question our Western view of nature as "natural resources" to be exploited. It was the right book at the right time.

I first picked up a small paperback edition of the *Tao Te Ching* around 1968, when I was a graduate student in physics at the University of Wisconsin. I had already noticed the parallels between the paradoxical logic of quantum physics and that of Zen as expressed in the writings of D. T. Suzuki and Alan Watts. (This was several years before the publication of Fritjof Capra's *The Tao of Physics*.)

With the *Tao Te Ching* now having been a part of my life for twenty-five years, both its wisdom and its mystery have seeped into my being. Or maybe more accurately, it has given me access to my own innate wisdom and sense of mystery. In my photographing I was intuitively going around and beyond words and seeing the ineffable, sometimes called Tao, through nature.

I especially delighted in creating photographs that teetered on the boundary between being and non-being—tree branches that delicately merge with the sky, fog almost obscuring a mountain, details of shells or grass that are almost unrecognizable. All this was for me a way to go beyond the too static "thingness" of ordinary consciousness, a doorway to a vastness that seemed to be my native land.

I still enjoy occasionally putting a roll of black-and-white film into my camera and wandering in nature, letting it speak to me as it did thirty years ago when I first started photographing. Back then, photography was the only way I knew of expressing the vastness of spirit that

I intuited. Now it is one of many ways, yet still a way I experience with great joy.

As an introduction to this edition of *Tao Te Ching*, writer, visionary artist, and cosmologist Rowena Pattee Kryder shows how the Tao transcends culture, how it brings a much needed unified perspective to the modern scientific world, and how it can inform many different spiritual practices.

In the back, a selection from Gia-fu's unpublished autobiography gives the flavor of his classical Chinese education. Then Tai Ji master Chungliang Al Huang discusses bringing this classical background to the West.

Finally, we hear from Toinette Lippe, our editor for all these years, about how the Tao was at work in the very publication of this book. Like the sage in the *Tao Te Ching* who ". . . works without recognition." (ch. 77), she was an integral, but not mentioned, part of the creation of this book. Her story is delightful!

At the very end is a brief list of Taoist resources in the United States.

—Jane English
Mount Shasta, California
April 1996

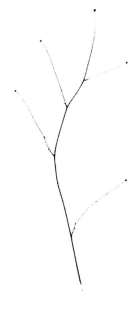

Tao means "The Way." The Tao is the Way to live in order to achieve by non-doing. This is a dynamic peace and mystery, neither passivity nor struggle. Tao is the everpresent eternal quality: source, law of creation, and fulfillment.

In modern times, as more people of different cultures meet one another because of our electronic and air travel networks, the "Way" can appear in many traditions and guises. The Taoist "Way" is not dependent on race, creed, or any cultural form. It is very fluid and mainly demands an openness to truth, the nameless mystery.

Taoism is associated with China, for Lao Tsu and Chuang Tsu brought forth the ancient "Way" through China five hundred years before Christ. Their works are the cultural foundations of traditional Taoism. The basic tenets are four: 1) that the "Way" of Tao underlies all things, 2) that human action that is harmonious with Tao is spontaneous, effortless, and inexhaustible, 3) that the perfected individual is a sage, free from desire and strife, and 4) that the sage conducts government by guiding his people back to a state of harmony with Tao.

The mystery of the "Way" can never be explained or named, but we can *live* it. No matter what we think, say, or do we are embraced by the "Way." Taoism uses the metaphor of water for the "Way," for it has innumerable forms and yet is always the same. It takes the form of mist and rain, underground wells and springs, rivulets and eddies, waterfalls and rivers, lakes and the great sea. The "Way" is infinitely compassionate, supporting and nurturing even in our ignorance, but we cannot truly be wholly nourished until we forgive ourselves our mistakes along the way and thus cease blaming others for our wounds. The Chinese *I Ching* says "no blame." The Lord's Prayer says similarly, "Forgive us our debts as we forgive our debtors." You may find other cultural manifestations of the "Way" that inspire you, that bring forth your essence, that enable you to take harmonious action with nature and spirit.

For the Taoist, nature and spirit interpenetrate. In spirit there is nature and in nature there is spirit.

The Islamic, Judaic, and Christian traditions tend to emphasize a greater separation of spirit and nature than cultures that are closer to shamanism, the aboriginal root of religions. Cultures that have a closer connection with shamanism include Taoism, Japanese Shinto and Zen, Amerindian "religions," and some forms of Tibetan Buddhism. With shamanic cultures, as with Taoism, spirit and nature, or God and creation, are inherently bound up with one another. The kabbalistic, Sufi, and mystical traditions of Judaism, Islam, and Christianity also have aspects of the awareness of the interpenetration of spirit and nature.

The separation of spirit and nature is based on the subject-object split, the great divide in consciousness that says sense perception and logical thought are objective whereas feeling and intuitive thought are subjective. In our scientifically oriented Western culture, objectivity is seen as the main criterion of truth, and subjectivity is considered personal and relative. But an insight, vision, or intuition may be more true than logic and description of objects. The test is the effectiveness of *living* the vision.

Once we lose the "Way" in this subject-object abyss, innumerable are the ills that grow out of it. The abuse of nature for technological exploitation, the resultant pollution, illnesses, and lack of wholesome food, water, and air for life are extreme signs of losing the "Way." God and the world seem to be antithetical because humans create culture in ignorance of spiritual and natural laws. Then supreme effort is required to return us to the "Way."

Being aware of our embodiment is the best opportunity to cultivate and refine ourselves to fulfill the purpose of reunion with the Tao. This reunion is not simply "spacing out" to some immortal realm, but grounding the "Way" right here and now on earth and in our bodies. It necessitates awareness of the earth as a living being, not inert matter to be exploited. As traditions break down we are forced to meet the "Way," which is both a mystery and a source for regenerative global culture. The essence of spiritual traditions can never be lost, for the "Way" is perennial wisdom, eternal truth.

There are innumerable teachings, doctrines, theologies, and practices of world religions to bring us to the "Way" if we have lost it. In the modern world we have the opportunity of distilling wisdom from these many traditions. We can meet the essentials and learn to resonate to spiritual dimensions that will inspire us to create holistic forms of education, ecological economies, visionary art, organic agriculture, and planetary governance.

The Tao, the "Way," is the eternal harmony of heaven, the human and earth in all times and places. It is ever renewed and yet inexhaustible. May you find your "Way" which is one with the eternal Tao.

—Rowena Pattee Kryder

Rowena Pattee Kryder is the founder of Creative Harmonics Institute in Mount Shasta, California, a center for meditation, shamanism, and sacred sciences and arts. She has produced several films and tapes and has exhibited her sacred art widely in the United States and Europe. Her many books include Gaia Matrix Oracle, Faces of the Moon Mother, Destiny, *and* Sacred Ground to Sacred Space.

TAO
TE
CHING

道可道非常道名可名非常名無名天地之始

有名萬物之母故常無欲以觀其妙

常有欲以觀其徼此兩者同出而異名

同謂之元元之又元眾妙之門

ONE

The Tao that can be told is not the eternal Tao.
The name that can be named is not the eternal name.
The nameless is the beginning of heaven and earth.
The named is the mother of ten thousand things.
Ever desireless, one can see the mystery.
Ever desiring, one can see the manifestations.
These two spring from the same source but differ in name;
    this appears as darkness.
Darkness within darkness.
The gate to all mystery.

TWO

Under heaven all can see beauty as beauty only because there is ugliness.
All can know good as good only because there is evil.

Therefore having and not having arise together.
Difficult and easy complement each other.
Long and short contrast each other;
High and low rest upon each other;
Voice and sound harmonize each other;
Front and back follow one another.

Therefore the sage goes about doing nothing, teaching no-talking.
The ten thousand things rise and fall without cease,
Creating, yet not possessing,
Working, yet not taking credit.
Work is done, then forgotten.
Therefore it lasts forever.

天下皆知美之為美斯惡已皆知善之為善斯不善已

故有無相生難易相成長短相較高下相傾音聲相和前後相隨

是以聖人處無為之事行不言之教萬物作焉而不辭

生而不有為而不恃功成而弗居

夫唯弗居是以不去

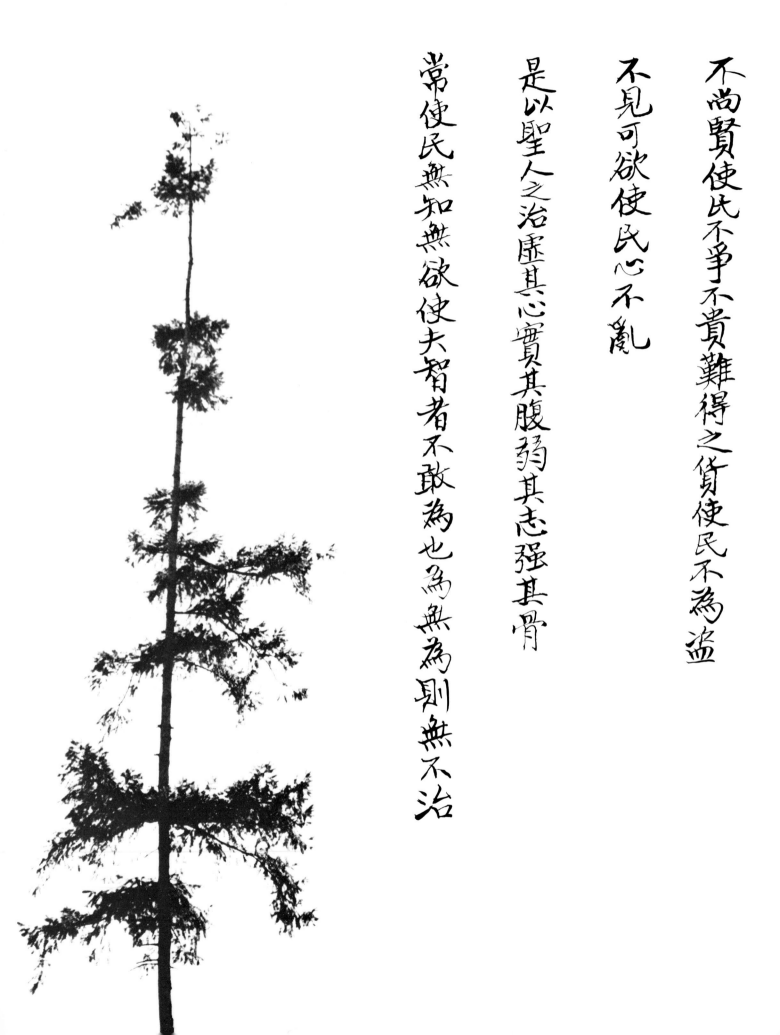

不尚賢使民不爭不貴難得之貨使民不為盜

不見可欲使民心不亂

是以聖人之治虛其心實其腹弱其志強其骨

常使民無知無欲使夫智者不敢為也為無為則無不治

THREE

Not exalting the gifted prevents quarreling.
Not collecting treasures prevents stealing.
Not seeing desirable things prevents confusion of the heart.

The wise therefore rule by emptying hearts and stuffing bellies,
    by weakening ambitions and strengthening bones.
If people lack knowledge and desire,
    then intellectuals will not try to interfere.
If nothing is done, then all will be well.

道沖而用之或不盈淵兮似萬物之宗挫其銳

解其紛和其光同其塵湛兮似或存

吾不知誰之子象帝之先

FOUR

The Tao is an empty vessel; it is used, but never filled.
Oh, unfathomable source of ten thousand things!
Blunt the sharpness,
Untangle the knot,
Soften the glare,
Merge with dust.
Oh, hidden deep but ever present!
I do not know from whence it comes.
It is the forefather of the emperors.

天地不仁以萬物為芻狗聖人不仁以百姓為芻狗

天地之間其猶橐籥乎虛而不屈動而愈出

多言數窮不如守中

FIVE

Heaven and earth are ruthless;
They see the ten thousand things as dummies.
The wise are ruthless;
They see the people as dummies.

The space between heaven and earth is like a bellows.
The shape changes but not the form;
The more it moves, the more it yields.
More words count less.
Hold fast to the center.

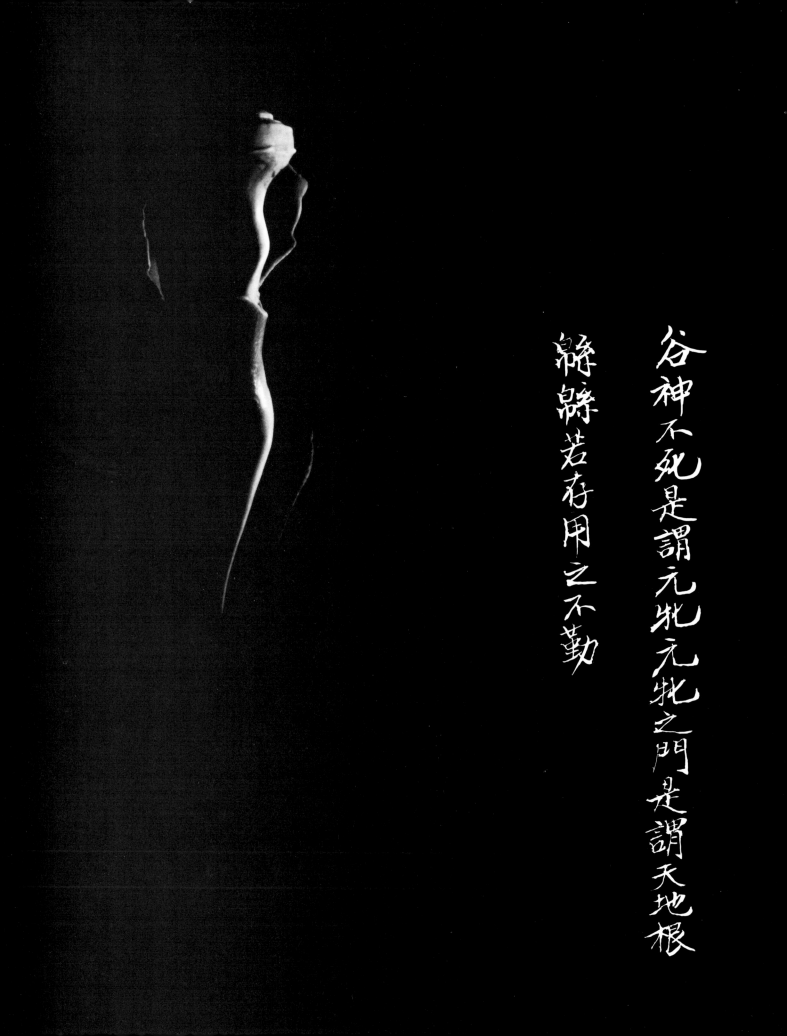

谷神不死是謂元牝元牝之門是謂天地根

緜緜若存用之不勤

SIX

The valley spirit never dies;
It is the woman, primal mother.
Her gateway is the root of heaven and earth.
It is like a veil barely seen.
Use it; it will never fail.

天長地久天地所以能長且久者以其不自生

故能長生是以聖人後其身而身先外其身而身存

非以其無私邪故能成其私

SEVEN

Heaven and earth last forever.
Why do heaven and earth last forever?
They are unborn,
So ever living.
The sage stays behind, thus he is ahead.
He is detached, thus at one with all.
Through selfless action, he attains fulfillment.

上善若水水善利萬物而不爭處眾人之所惡

故幾於道居善地心善淵與善仁言善信正善治

事善能動善時夫唯不爭故無尤

EIGHT

The highest good is like water.
Water gives life to the ten thousand things and does not strive.
It flows in places men reject and so is like the Tao.

In dwelling, be close to the land.
In meditation, go deep in the heart.
In dealing with others, be gentle and kind.
In speech, be true.
In ruling, be just.
In business, be competent.
In action, watch the timing.

No fight: No blame.

持而盈之不如其已揣而梲之不可長保

金玉滿堂莫之能守富貴而驕自遺其咎

功遂身退天之道

NINE

Better stop short than fill to the brim.
Oversharpen the blade, and the edge will soon blunt.
Amass a store of gold and jade, and no one can protect it.
Claim wealth and titles, and disaster will follow.
Retire when the work is done.
This is the way of heaven.

載營魄抱一能無離乎專氣致柔能嬰兒乎

滌除元覽能無疵乎愛民治國能無知乎

天門開闔能無雌乎明白四達能無為乎

生之畜之生而不有為而不恃

長而不宰是謂元德

TEN

Carrying body and soul and embracing the one,
Can you avoid separation?
Attending fully and becoming supple,
Can you be as a newborn babe?
Washing and cleansing the primal vision,
Can you be without stain?
Loving all men and ruling the country,
Can you be without cleverness?
Opening and closing the gates of heaven,
Can you play the role of woman?
Understanding and being open to all things,
Are you able to do nothing?
Giving birth and nourishing,
Bearing yet not possessing,
Working yet not taking credit,
Leading yet not dominating,
This is the Primal Virtue.

三十輻共一轂當其無有車之用

埏埴以為器當其無有器之用

鑿戶牖以為室當其無有室之用

故有之以為利無之以為用

ELEVEN

Thirty spokes share the wheel's hub;
It is the center hole that makes it useful.
Shape clay into a vessel;
It is the space within that makes it useful.
Cut doors and windows for a room;
It is the holes which make it useful.
Therefore profit comes from what is there;
Usefulness from what is not there.

TWELVE

The five colors blind the eye.
The five tones deafen the ear.
The five flavors dull the taste.
Racing and hunting madden the mind.
Precious things lead one astray.

Therefore the sage is guided by what he feels and not by what he sees.
He lets go of that and chooses this.

五色令人目盲五音令人耳聾五味令人口爽

馳騁畋獵令人心發狂難得之貨令人行妨

是以聖人為腹不為目

故去彼取此

寵辱若驚貴大患若身

何謂寵辱若驚寵為下得之若驚失之若驚是謂寵辱若驚

何謂貴大患若身吾所以有大患者為吾有身及吾無身吾有何患

故貴以身為天下若可寄天下愛以身為天下若可託天下

THIRTEEN

Accept disgrace willingly.
Accept misfortune as the human condition.

What do you mean by "Accept disgrace willingly"?
Accept being unimportant.
Do not be concerned with loss or gain.
This is called "accepting disgrace willingly."

What do you mean by "Accept misfortune as the human condition"?
Misfortune comes from having a body.
Without a body, how could there be misfortune?

Surrender yourself humbly; then you can be trusted to care for all things.
Love the world as your own self; then you can truly care for all things.

FOURTEEN

Look, it cannot be seen—it is beyond form.
Listen, it cannot be heard—it is beyond sound.
Grasp, it cannot be held—it is intangible.
These three are indefinable;
Therefore they are joined in one.

From above it is not bright;
From below it is not dark:
An unbroken thread beyond description.
It returns to nothingness.
The form of the formless,
The image of the imageless,
It is called indefinable and beyond imagination.

Stand before it and there is no beginning.
Follow it and there is no end.
Stay with the ancient Tao,
Move with the present.

Knowing the ancient beginning is the essence of Tao.

視之不見名曰夷聽之不聞名曰希搏之不得名曰微

此三者不可致詰故混而為一其上不皦其下不昧

繩繩不可名復歸於無物是謂無狀之狀無物之象是謂惚恍

迎之不見其首隨之不見其後

執古之道以御今之有能知古始是謂道紀

古之善為士者微妙元通深不可識

夫唯不可識故強為之容

豫焉若冬涉川猶兮若畏四鄰儼兮其若客

渙兮若冰之將釋敦兮其若樸曠兮其若谷

混兮其若濁孰能濁以靜之徐清孰能安以久動之徐生

保此道者不欲盈夫唯不盈故能蔽不新成

FIFTEEN

The ancient masters were subtle, mysterious, profound, responsive.
The depth of their knowledge is unfathomable.
Because it is unfathomable,
All we can do is describe their appearance.
Watchful, like men crossing a winter stream.
Alert, like men aware of danger.
Courteous, like visiting guests.
Yielding, like ice about to melt.
Simple, like uncarved blocks of wood.
Hollow, like caves.
Opaque, like muddy pools.

Who can wait quietly while the mud settles?
Who can remain still until the moment of action?
Observers of the Tao do not seek fulfillment.
Not seeking fulfillment, they are not swayed by desire for change.

致虛極守靜篤萬物並作吾以觀復夫物芸芸各復歸其根

歸根曰靜是謂復命復命曰常知常曰明

不知常妄作凶知常容容乃公公乃王

王乃天天乃道道乃久沒身不殆

SIXTEEN

Empty yourself of everything.
Let the mind rest at peace.
The ten thousand things rise and fall while the Self watches their return.
They grow and flourish and then return to the source.
Returning to the source is stillness, which is the way of nature.
The way of nature is unchanging.
Knowing constancy is insight.
Not knowing constancy leads to disaster.
Knowing constancy, the mind is open.
With an open mind, you will be openhearted.
Being openhearted, you will act royally.
Being royal, you will attain the divine.
Being divine, you will be at one with the Tao.
Being at one with the Tao is eternal.
And though the body dies, the Tao will never pass away.

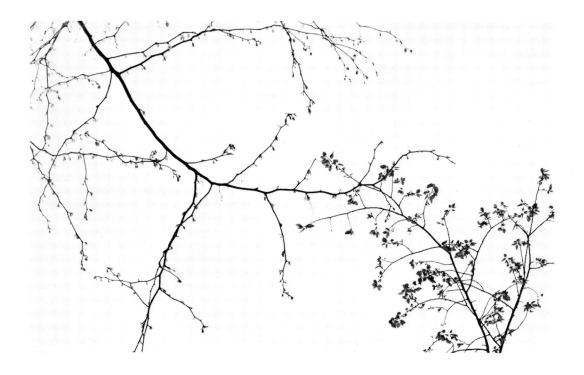

SEVENTEEN

The very highest is barely known by men.
Then comes that which they know and love,
Then that which is feared,
Then that which is despised.

He who does not trust enough will not be trusted.

When actions are performed
Without unnecessary speech,
People say, "We did it!"

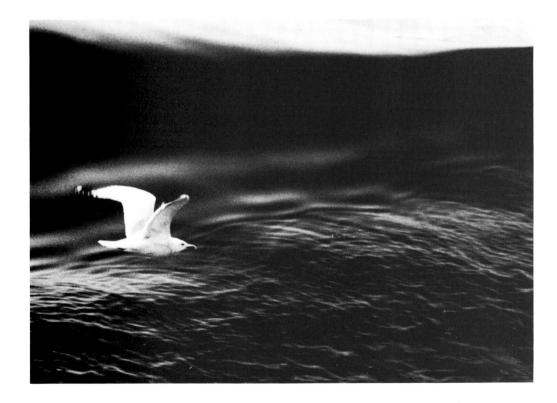

太上下知有之其次親而譽之
其次畏之其次侮之
信不足焉有不信焉
悠今其貴言功成事遂百姓皆謂我自然

一

一

大道廢有仁義慧智出有大偽
六親不和有孝慈國家昏亂有忠臣

EIGHTEEN

When the great Tao is forgotten,
Kindness and morality arise.
When wisdom and intelligence are born,
The great pretense begins.

When there is no peace within the family,
Filial piety and devotion arise.
When the country is confused and in chaos,
Loyal ministers appear.

絶聖棄智民利百倍

絶仁棄義民復孝慈絶巧棄利盗賊無有

此三者以為文不足故令有所屬見素抱樸少私寡欲

NINETEEN

Give up sainthood, renounce wisdom,
And it will be a hundred times better for everyone.

Give up kindness, renounce morality,
And men will rediscover filial piety and love.

Give up ingenuity, renounce profit,
And bandits and thieves will disappear.

These three are outward forms alone; they are not sufficient in themselves.
It is more important
To see the simplicity,
To realize one's true nature,
To cast off selfishness
And temper desire.

絕學無憂唯之與阿相去幾何善之與惡相去若何

人之所畏不可不畏荒兮其未央哉

眾人熙熙如享太牢如春登臺我獨泊兮其未兆

如嬰兒之未孩儽儽兮若無所歸眾人皆有餘而我獨若遺

我愚人之心也哉沌沌兮俗人昭昭我獨昏昏

俗人察察我獨悶悶澹兮其若海飂兮若無止

眾人皆有以而我獨頑似鄙我獨異於人而貴食母

TWENTY

Give up learning, and put an end to your troubles.

Is there a difference between yes and no?
Is there a difference between good and evil?
Must I fear what others fear? What nonsense!
Other people are contented, enjoying the sacrificial feast of the ox.
In spring some go to the park, and climb the terrace,
But I alone am drifting, not knowing where I am.
Like a newborn babe before it learns to smile,
I am alone, without a place to go.

Others have more than they need, but I alone have nothing.
I am a fool. Oh, yes! I am confused.
Other men are clear and bright,
But I alone am dim and weak.
Other men are sharp and clever,
But I alone am dull and stupid.
Oh, I drift like the waves of the sea,
Without direction, like the restless wind.

Everyone else is busy,
But I alone am aimless and depressed.
I am different.
I am nourished by the great mother.

孔德之容惟道是從道之為物惟恍惟惚

惚兮恍兮其中有象恍兮惚兮其中有物

窈兮冥兮其中有精其精甚真其中有信

自古及今其名不去以閱眾甫

吾何以知眾甫之狀哉以此

TWENTY-ONE

The greatest Virtue is to follow Tao and Tao alone.
The Tao is elusive and intangible.
Oh, it is intangible and elusive, and yet within is image.
Oh, it is elusive and intangible, and yet within is form.
Oh, it is dim and dark, and yet within is essence.
This essence is very real, and therein lies faith.
From the very beginning until now its name has never been forgotten.
Thus I perceive the creation.
How do I know the ways of creation?
Because of this.

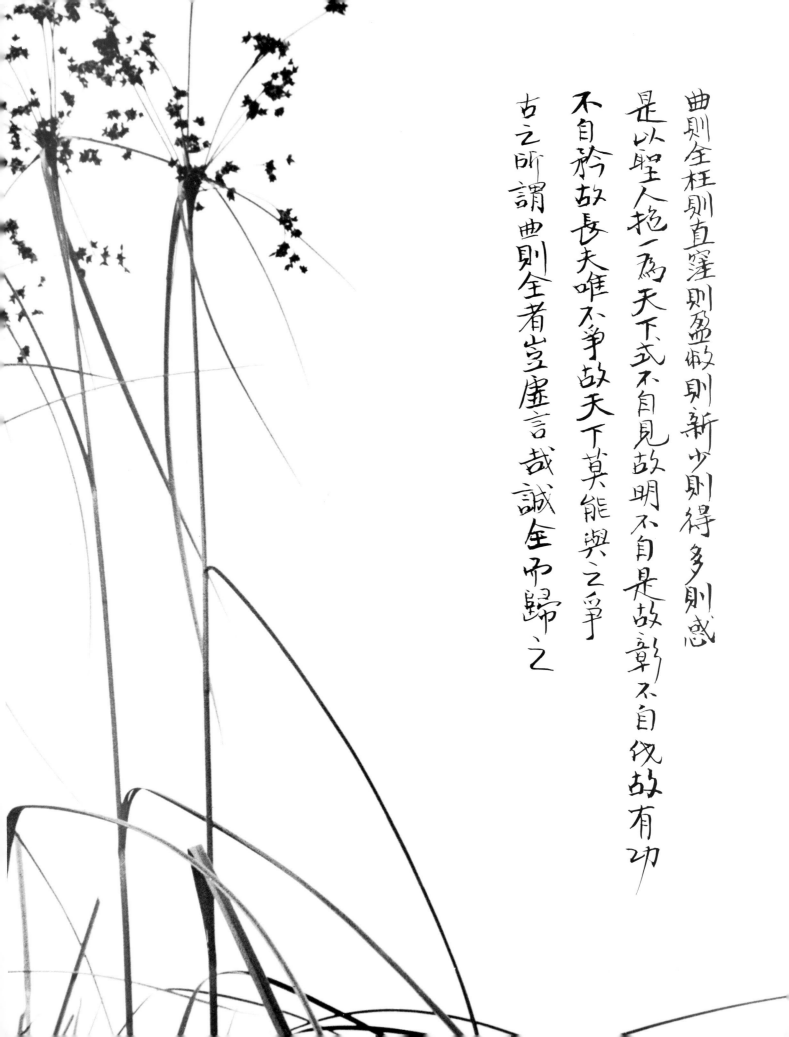

曲則全枉則直窪則盈敝則新少則得多則惑

是以聖人抱一為天下式不自見故明不自是故彰不自伐故有功

不自矜故長夫唯不爭故天下莫能與之爭

古之所謂曲則全者豈虛言哉誠全而歸之

TWENTY-TWO

Yield and overcome;
Bend and be straight;
Empty and be full;
Wear out and be new;
Have little and gain;
Have much and be confused.

Therefore wise men embrace the one
And set an example to all.
Not putting on a display,
They shine forth.
Not justifying themselves,
They are distinguished.
Not boasting,
They receive recognition.
Not bragging,
They never falter.
They do not quarrel,
So no one quarrels with them.
Therefore the ancients say, "Yield and overcome."
Is that an empty saying?
Be really whole,
And all things will come to you.

TWENTY-THREE

To talk little is natural.
High winds do not last all morning.
Heavy rain does not last all day.
Why is this? Heaven and earth!
If heaven and earth cannot make things eternal,
How is it possible for man?

He who follows the Tao
Is at one with the Tao.
He who is virtuous
Experiences Virtue.
He who loses the way
Feels lost.
When you are at one with the Tao,
The Tao welcomes you.
When you are at one with Virtue,
The Virtue is always there.
When you are at one with loss,
The loss is experienced willingly.

He who does not trust enough
Will not be trusted.

希言自然故飄風不終朝驟雨不終日孰為此者天地

天地尚不能久而況於人乎

故從事於道者道者同於德德者同於失失者同於失

同於道者道亦樂得之同於德者德亦樂得之

同於失者失亦樂得之信不足焉有不信焉

企者不立跨者不行自見者不明
自是者不彰自伐者無功
自矜者不長其在道也曰
餘食贅行物或惡之故有道者不処

TWENTY-FOUR

He who stands on tiptoe is not steady.
He who strides cannot maintain the pace.
He who makes a show is not enlightened.
He who is self-righteous is not respected.
He who boasts achieves nothing.
He who brags will not endure.
According to followers of the Tao,
    "These are extra food and unnecessary luggage."
They do not bring happiness.
Therefore followers of the Tao avoid them.

有物混成先天地生
寂兮寥兮獨立不改周行而不殆可以為天下母
吾不知其名字之曰「道」強為之名曰大
大曰逝逝曰遠遠曰反故「道」大天大地大王亦大
域中有四大而王居其一焉人法地地法天天法「道」「道」法自然

TWENTY-FIVE

Something mysteriously formed,
Born before heaven and earth.
In the silence and the void,
Standing alone and unchanging,
Ever present and in motion.
Perhaps it is the mother of ten thousand things.
I do not know its name.
Call it Tao.
For lack of a better word, I call it great.

Being great, it flows.
It flows far away.
Having gone far, it returns.

Therefore, "Tao is great;
Heaven is great;
Earth is great;
The king is also great."
These are the four great powers
    of the universe,
And the king is one of them.

Man follows the earth.
Earth follows heaven.
Heaven follows the Tao.
Tao follows what is natural.

重為輕根靜為躁君

是以聖人終日行不離輜重雖有榮觀燕處超然

奈何萬乘之主而以身輕天下輕則失本躁則失君

TWENTY-SIX

The heavy is the root of the light;
The still is the master of unrest.

Therefore the sage, traveling all day,
Does not lose sight of his baggage.
Though there are beautiful things to be seen,
He remains unattached and calm.

Why should the lord of ten thousand chariots act lightly in public?
To be light is to lose one's root.
To be restless is to lose one's control.

TWENTY-SEVEN

A good walker leaves no tracks;
A good speaker makes no slips;
A good reckoner needs no tally.
A good door needs no lock,
Yet no one can open it.
Good binding requires no knots,
Yet no one can loosen it.

Therefore the sage takes care of all men
And abandons no one.
He takes care of all things
And abandons nothing.

This is called "following the light."

What is a good man?
A teacher of a bad man.
What is a bad man?
A good man's charge.
If the teacher is not respected,
And the student not cared for,
Confusion will arise, however clever one is.
This is the crux of mystery.

善行無轍迹善言無瑕謫善數不用籌策

善閉無關楗而不可開善結無繩約而不可解

是以聖人常善救人故無棄人常善救物故無棄物

是謂龍花眠故善人者不善人之師

不善人者善人之資不貴其師

不愛其資雖智大迷是謂要妙

知其雄守其雌為天下谿為天下谿常德不離復歸於嬰兒

知其白守其黑為天下式為天下式常德不忒復歸於無極

知其榮守其辱為天下谷為天下谷常德乃足復歸於樸

樸散則為器聖人用之則為官長故大制不割

TWENTY-EIGHT

Know the strength of man,
But keep a woman's care!
Be the stream of the universe!
Being the stream of the universe,
Ever true and unswerving,
Become as a little child once more.

Know the white,
But keep the black!
Be an example to the world!
Being an example to the world,
Ever true and unwavering,
Return to the infinite.

Know honor,
Yet keep humility.
Be the valley of the universe!
Being the valley of the universe,
Ever true and resourceful,
Return to the state of the uncarved block.

When the block is carved, it becomes useful.
When the sage uses it, he becomes the ruler.
Thus, "A great tailor cuts little."

TWENTY-NINE

Do you think you can take over the universe and improve it?
I do not believe it can be done.

The universe is sacred.
You cannot improve it.
If you try to change it, you will ruin it.
If you try to hold it, you will lose it.

So sometimes things are ahead and sometimes they are behind;
Sometimes breathing is hard, sometimes it comes easily;
Sometimes there is strength and sometimes weakness;
Sometimes one is up and sometimes down.

Therefore the sage avoids extremes, excesses, and complacency.

是以聖人去甚去奢去泰

故物或行或隨或歔或吹或強或羸或挫或隳

天下神器不可為也為者敗之執者失之

將欲取天下而為之吾見其不得已

以道佐人主者不以兵強天下其事好還
師之所處荊棘生焉大軍之後必有凶年善有果而已不敢以取強
果而勿矜果而勿伐果而勿驕果而不得已果而勿強
物壯則老是謂不道不道早已

THIRTY

Whenever you advise a ruler in the way of Tao,
Counsel him not to use force to conquer the universe.
For this would only cause resistance.
Thorn bushes spring up wherever the army has passed.
Lean years follow in the wake of a great war.
Just do what needs to be done.
Never take advantage of power.

Achieve results,
But never glory in them.
Achieve results,
But never boast.
Achieve results,
But never be proud.
Achieve results,
Because this is the natural way.
Achieve results,
But not through violence.

Force is followed by loss of strength.
This is not the way of Tao.
That which goes against the Tao
        comes to an early end.

夫佳兵者不祥之器物或惡之故有道者不處

君子居則貴左用兵則貴右兵者不祥之器非君子之器

不得已而用之恬淡為上勝而不美而美之者是樂殺人

夫樂殺人者則不可以得志於天下矣吉事尚左凶事尚右

偏將軍居左上將軍居右言以喪禮處之

殺人之眾以哀悲泣之戰勝以喪禮處之

THIRTY-ONE

Good weapons are instruments of fear; all creatures hate them.
Therefore followers of Tao never use them.
The wise man prefers the left.
The man of war prefers the right.

Weapons are instruments of fear; they are not a wise man's tools.
He uses them only when he has no choice.
Peace and quiet are dear to his heart,
And victory no cause for rejoicing.
If you rejoice in victory, then you delight in killing;
If you delight in killing, you cannot fulfill yourself.

On happy occasions precedence is given to the left,
On sad occasions to the right.
In the army the general stands on the left,
The commander-in-chief on the right.
This means that war is conducted like a funeral.
When many people are being killed,
They should be mourned in heartfelt sorrow.
That is why a victory must be observed like a funeral.

道常無名樸雖小天下莫能臣也侯王若能守之萬物將自賓

天地相合以降甘露民莫之令而自均

始制有名名亦既有夫亦將知止知止可以不殆

譬道之在天下猶川谷之於江海

THIRTY-TWO

The Tao is forever undefined.
Small though it is in the unformed state, it cannot be grasped.
If kings and lords could harness it,
The ten thousand things would naturally obey.
Heaven and earth would come together
And gentle rain fall.
Men would need no more instruction
      and all things would take their course.

Once the whole is divided, the parts need names.
There are already enough names.
One must know when to stop.
Knowing when to stop averts trouble.
Tao in the world is like a river flowing home to the sea.

知人者智　自知者明　勝人者有力　自勝者強
知足者富　強行者有志　不失其所者久　死而不亡者壽

THIRTY-THREE

Knowing others is wisdom;
Knowing the self is enlightenment.
Mastering others requires force;
Mastering the self needs strength.

He who knows he has enough is rich.
Perseverance is a sign of will power.
He who stays where he is endures.
To die but not to perish is to be eternally present.

大道汎兮其可左右萬物恃之而生而不辭功成不名有

衣養萬物而不為主常無欲可名於小

萬物歸焉而不為主可名為大

以其終不自為大故能成其大

THIRTY-FOUR

The great Tao flows everywhere, both to the left and to the right.
The ten thousand things depend upon it; it holds nothing back.
It fulfills its purpose silently and makes no claim.

It nourishes the ten thousand things,
And yet is not their lord.
It has no aim; it is very small.

The ten thousand things return to it,
Yet it is not their lord.
It is very great.

It does not show greatness,
And is therefore truly great.

執大象天下往往而不害安平太樂與餌過客止

道之出口淡乎其無味視之不足見聽之不足聞用之不足既

THIRTY-FIVE

All men will come to him who keeps to the one,
For there lie rest and happiness and peace.

Passersby may stop for music and good food,
But a description of the Tao
Seems without substance or flavor.
It cannot be seen, it cannot be heard,
And yet it cannot be exhausted.

THIRTY-SIX

That which shrinks
Must first expand.
That which fails
Must first be strong.
That which is cast down
Must first be raised.
Before receiving
There must be giving.

This is called perception of the nature of things.
Soft and weak overcome hard and strong.

Fish cannot leave deep waters,
And a country's weapons should not be displayed.

道常無為而無不為侯王若能守之
萬物將自化化而欲作吾將鎮之以無名之樸
無名之樸夫亦將無欲不欲以靜天下將自定

THIRTY-SEVEN

Tao abides in non-action,
Yet nothing is left undone.
If kings and lords observed this,
The ten thousand things would develop naturally.
If they still desired to act,
They would return to the simplicity of formless substance.
Without form there is no desire.
Without desire there is tranquillity.
And in this way all things would be at peace.

上德不德是以有德下德不失德是以無德

上德無為而無以為下德為之而有以為

上仁為之而無以為上義為之而有以為上禮為之而莫之應則攘臂而扔之

故失道而後德失德而後仁失仁而後義失義而後禮夫禮者忠信之薄而亂之首

前識者道之華而愚之始是以大丈夫處其厚不居其薄處其實不居其華

故去彼取此

THIRTY-EIGHT

A truly good man is not aware of his goodness,
And is therefore good.
A foolish man tries to be good,
And is therefore not good.

A truly good man does nothing,
Yet leaves nothing undone.
A foolish man is always doing,
Yet much remains to be done.

When a truly kind man does something, he leaves nothing undone.
When a just man does something, he leaves a great deal to be done.
When a disciplinarian does something and no one responds,
He rolls up his sleeves in an attempt to enforce order.

Therefore when Tao is lost, there is goodness.
When goodness is lost, there is kindness.
When kindness is lost, there is justice.
When justice is lost, there is ritual.
Now ritual is the husk of faith and loyalty, the beginning of confusion.
Knowledge of the future is only a flowery trapping of Tao.
It is the beginning of folly.

Therefore the truly great man dwells on what is real
        and not what is on the surface,
On the fruit and not the flower.
Therefore accept the one and reject the other.

昔之得一者天得以清地得以寧神得以靈谷得

一以盈萬物得以生侯王得以為天下貞

其致之天無以清將恐裂地無以寧將恐蔡神無以靈將恐歇谷無以盈將恐竭

萬物無以生將恐滅侯王無以貴高將恐蹶故貴以賤為本高以下為基

是以侯王自謂孤寡不穀此非以賤為本邪非乎故致數輿無輿不欲琭琭如玉珞珞如石

THIRTY-NINE

These things from ancient times arise from one:
The sky is whole and clear.
The earth is whole and firm.
The spirit is whole and strong.
The valley is whole and full.
The ten thousand things are whole and alive.
Kings and lords are whole, and the country is upright.
All these are in virtue of wholeness.

The clarity of the sky prevents its falling.
The firmness of the earth prevents its splitting.
The strength of the spirit prevents its being used up.
The fullness of the valley prevents its running dry.
The growth of the ten thousand things prevents their dying out.
The leadership of kings and lords prevents the downfall
    of the country.

Therefore the humble is the root of the noble.
The low is the foundation of the high.
Princes and lords consider themselves
    "orphaned," "widowed," and "worthless."
Do they not depend on being humble?

Too much success is not an advantage.
Do not tinkle like jade
Or clatter like stone chimes.

FORTY

Returning is the motion of the Tao.
Yielding is the way of the Tao.
The ten thousand things are born of being.
Being is born of not being.

反者道之動弱者道之用
天下萬物生於有有生於無

FORTY-ONE

The wise student hears of the Tao and practices it diligently.
The average student hears of the Tao and gives it thought now and again.
The foolish student hears of the Tao and laughs aloud.
If there were no laughter, the Tao would not be what it is.

Hence it is said:
The bright path seems dim;
Going forward seems like retreat;
The easy way seems hard;
The highest Virtue seems empty;
Great purity seems sullied;
A wealth of Virtue seems inadequate;
The strength of Virtue seems frail;
Real Virtue seems unreal;
The perfect square has no corners;
Great talents ripen late;
The highest notes are hard to hear;
The greatest form has no shape.
The Tao is hidden and without name.
The Tao alone nourishes and brings everything to fulfillment.

上士聞道勤而行之中士聞道若存若亡下士聞道大笑之不笑不足以為道

故建言有之明道若昧進道若退夷道若纇上德若谷

大白若辱廣德若不足建德若偷質真若渝

大方無隅大器晚成大音希聲大象無形

道隱無名夫唯道善貸且成

道生一一生二二生三三生万物万物負陰而抱陽沖氣以為和

人之所惡唯孤寡不穀而王公以為稱故物或損之而益或益之而損

人之所教我亦教之強梁者不得其死吾將以為教父

FORTY-TWO

The Tao begot one.
One begot two.
Two begot three.
And three begot the ten thousand things.

The ten thousand things carry yin and embrace yang.
They achieve harmony by combining these forces.

Men hate to be "orphaned," "widowed," or "worthless,"
But this is how kings and lords describe themselves.

For one gains by losing
And loses by gaining.

What others teach, I also teach; that is:
"A violent man will die a violent death!"
This will be the essence of my teaching.

FORTY-THREE

The softest thing in the universe
Overcomes the hardest thing in the universe.
That without substance can enter where there is no room.
Hence I know the value of non-action.

Teaching without words and work without doing
Are understood by very few.

天下之至柔馳騁天下之至堅無有入無間

吾是以知無為之有益

不言之教無為之益天下希及之

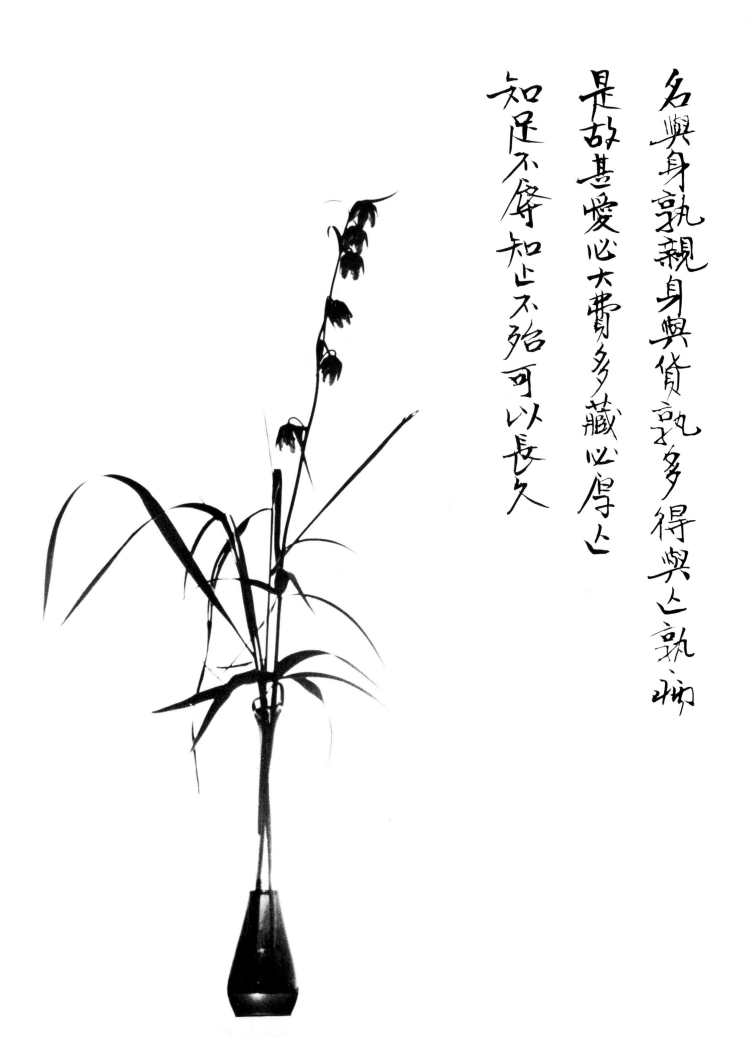

名與身孰親身與貨孰多得與亡孰病

是故甚愛必大費多藏必厚亡

知足不辱知止不殆可以長久

FORTY-FOUR

Fame or self: Which matters more?
Self or wealth: Which is more precious?
Gain or loss: Which is more painful?

He who is attached to things will suffer much.
He who saves will suffer heavy loss.
A contented man is never disappointed.
He who knows when to stop does not find himself in trouble.
He will stay forever safe.

FORTY-FIVE

Great accomplishment seems imperfect,
Yet it does not outlive its usefulness.
Great fullness seems empty,
Yet it cannot be exhausted.

Great straightness seems twisted.
Great intelligence seems stupid.
Great eloquence seems awkward.

Movement overcomes cold.
Stillness overcomes heat.
Stillness and tranquillity set things in order in the universe.

大成若缺其用不弊大盈若沖其用不窮

大直若屈大巧若拙大辯若訥

躁勝寒靜勝熱清靜為天下正

不出戶知天下不闚牖見天道其出彌遠其知彌少

以是聖人不行而知不見而名不為而成

FORTY-SEVEN

Without going outside, you may know the whole world.
Without looking through the window, you may see the ways of heaven.
The farther you go, the less you know.

Thus the sage knows without traveling;
He sees without looking;
He works without doing.

為學日益為道日損

損之又損以至於無為無為而無不為

取天下常以無事及其有事不足以取天下

FORTY-EIGHT

In the pursuit of learning, every day something is acquired.
In the pursuit of Tao, every day something is dropped.

Less and less is done
Until non-action is achieved.
When nothing is done, nothing is left undone.

The world is ruled by letting things take their course.
It cannot be ruled by interfering.

FORTY-NINE

The sage has no mind of his own.
He is aware of the needs of others.

I am good to people who are good.
I am also good to people who are not good.
Because Virtue is goodness.
I have faith in people who are faithful.
I also have faith in people who are not faithful.
Because Virtue is faithfulness.

The sage is shy and humble—to the world he seems confusing.
Men look to him and listen.
He behaves like a little child.

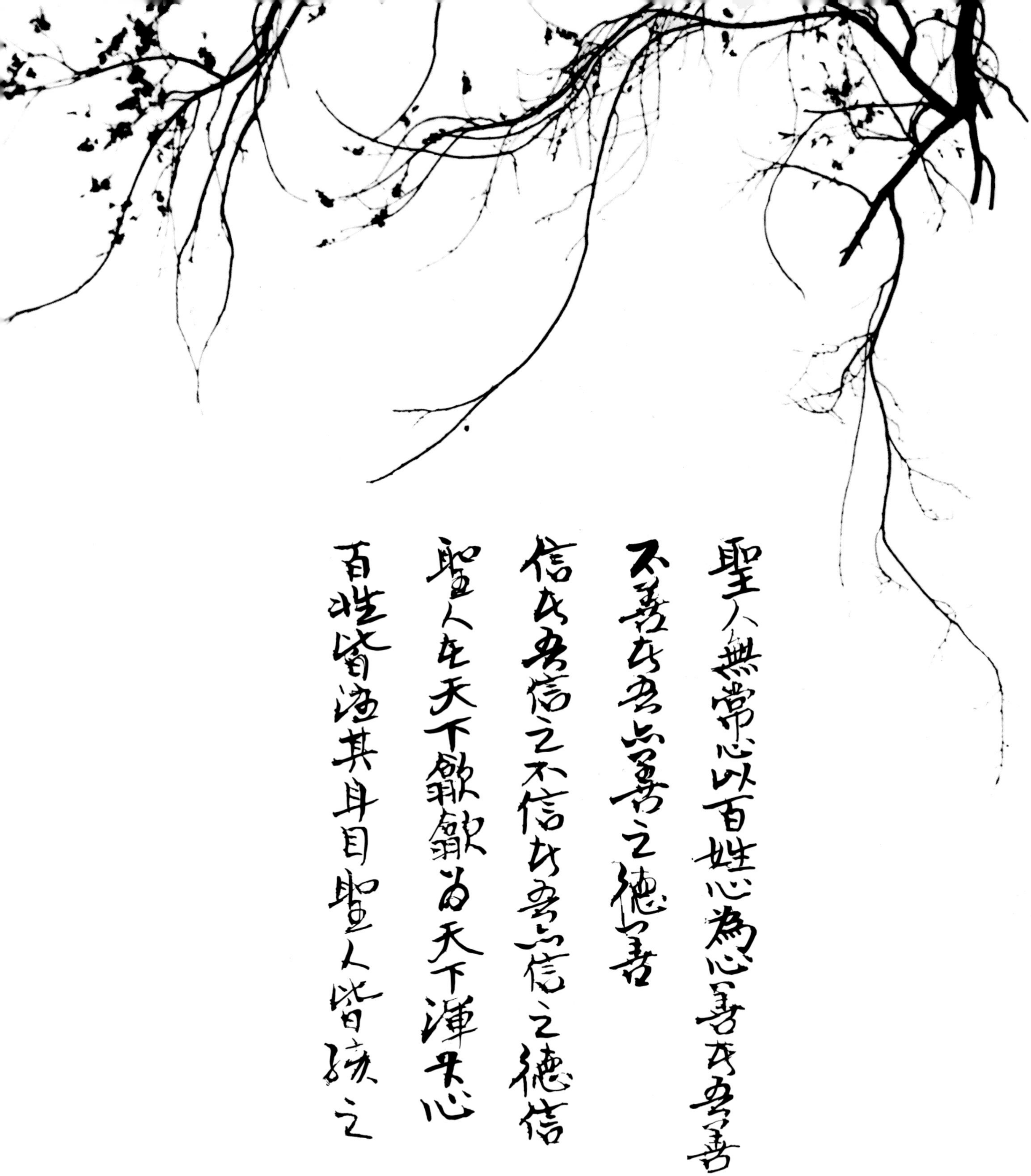

聖人無常心以百姓心為心善者吾善之

不善者吾亦善之德善

信者吾信之不信者吾亦信之德信

聖人在天下歙歙為天下渾其心

百姓皆注其耳目聖人皆孩之

FIFTY

Between birth and death,
Three in ten are followers of life,
Three in ten are followers of death,
And men just passing from birth to death also number three in ten.
Why is this so?
Because they live their lives on the gross level.

He who knows how to live can walk abroad
Without fear of rhinoceros or tiger.
He will not be wounded in battle.
For in him rhinoceroses can find no place to thrust their horn,
Tigers no place to use their claws,
And weapons no place to pierce.
Why is this so?
Because he has no place for death to enter.

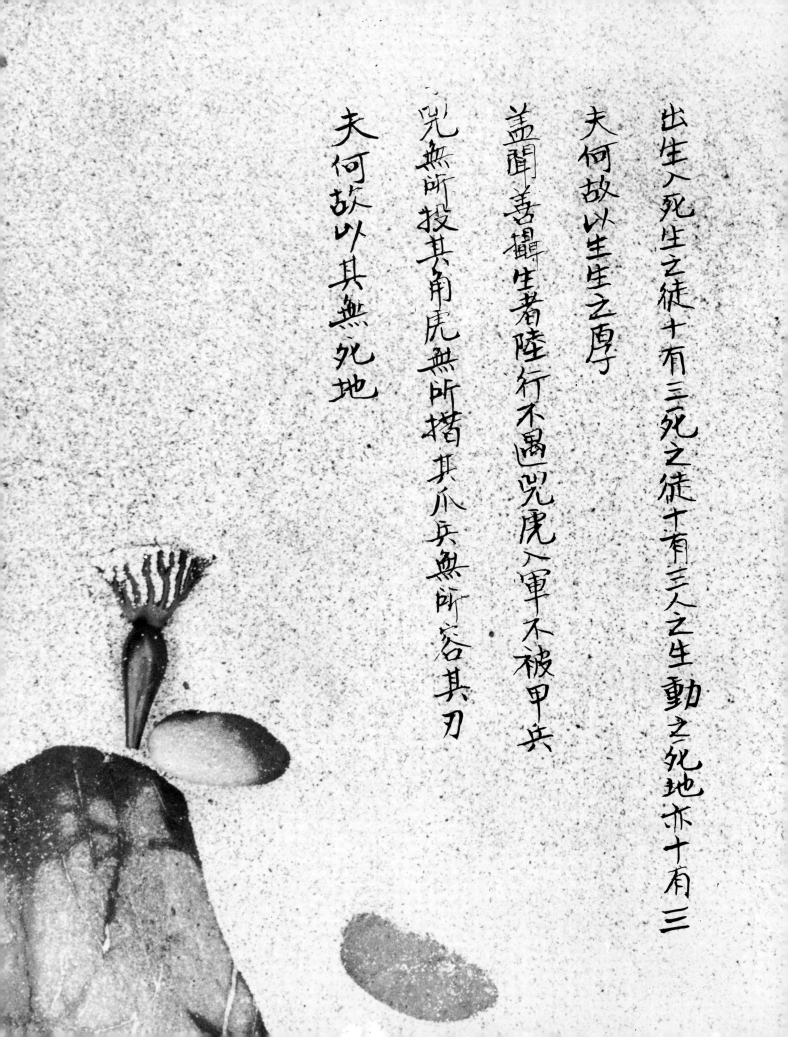

出生入死生之徒十有三死之徒十有三人之生動之死地亦十有三

夫何故以生生之厚

蓋聞善攝生者陸行不遇兕虎入軍不被甲兵

兕無所投其角虎無所措其爪兵無所容其刃

夫何故以其無死地

道生之德畜之物形之勢成之

是以万物莫不尊道而貴德

道之尊德之貴夫莫之命而常自然

故道生之德畜之長之育之亭之毒之養之覆之

生而不有為而不恃長而不宰是謂元德

FIFTY-ONE

All things arise from Tao.
They are nourished by Virtue.
They are formed from matter.
They are shaped by environment.
Thus the ten thousand things all respect Tao and honor Virtue.
Respect of Tao and honor of Virtue are not demanded,
But they are in the nature of things.

Therefore all things arise from Tao.
By Virtue they are nourished,
Developed, cared for,
Sheltered, comforted,
Grown, and protected.
Creating without claiming,
Doing without taking credit,
Guiding without interfering,
This is Primal Virtue.

天下有始以為天下母既知其母以知其子既知其子復守其母
沒身不殆塞其兌閉其門終身不動開其兌濟其事終身不救
見小曰明守柔曰強用其光復歸其明無遺身殃是為習常

FIFTY-TWO

The beginning of the universe
Is the mother of all things.
Knowing the mother, one also knows the sons.
Knowing the sons, yet remaining in touch with the mother,
Brings freedom from the fear of death.

Keep your mouth shut,
Guard the senses,
And life is ever full.
Open your mouth,
Always be busy,
And life is beyond hope.

Seeing the small is insight;
Yielding to force is strength.
Using the outer light, return to insight,
And in this way be saved from harm.
This is learning constancy.

使我介然有知行於大道唯施是畏

大道甚夷而民好徑

朝甚除田甚蕪倉甚虛服文綵帶利劍厭飲食

財貨有餘是謂盜夸非道也哉

FIFTY-THREE

If I have even just a little sense,
I will walk on the main road and my only fear will be of straying from it.
Keeping to the main road is easy,
But people love to be sidetracked.

When the court is arrayed in splendor,
The fields are full of weeds,
And the granaries are bare.
Some wear gorgeous clothes,
Carry sharp swords,
And indulge themselves with food and drink;
They have more possessions than they can use.
They are robber barons.
This is certainly not the way of Tao.

FIFTY-FOUR

What is firmly established cannot be uprooted.
What is firmly grasped cannot slip away.
It will be honored from generation to generation.

Cultivate Virtue in your self,
And Virtue will be real.
Cultivate it in the family,
And Virtue will abound.
Cultivate it in the village,
And Virtue will grow.
Cultivate it in the nation,
And Virtue will be abundant.
Cultivate it in the universe,
And Virtue will be everywhere.

Therefore look at the body as body;
Look at the family as family;
Look at the village as village;
Look at the nation as nation;
Look at the universe as universe.

How do I know the universe is like this?
By looking!

善建者不拔 善抱者不脫 子孫以祭祀不輟
修之於身其德乃真 修之於家其德乃餘
修之於鄉其德乃長 修之於國其德乃豐
修之於天下其德乃普
故以身觀身 以家觀家 以鄉觀鄉 以國觀國
以天下觀天下
吾何以知天下然哉 以此

FIFTY-FIVE

He who is filled with Virtue is like a newborn child.
Wasps and serpents will not sting him;
Wild beasts will not pounce upon him;
He will not be attacked by birds of prey.
His bones are soft, his muscles weak,
But his grip is firm.
He has not experienced the union of man and woman, but is whole.
His manhood is strong.
He screams all day without becoming hoarse.
This is perfect harmony.

Knowing harmony is constancy.
Knowing constancy is enlightenment.

It is not wise to rush about.
Controlling the breath causes strain.
If too much energy is used, exhaustion follows.
This is not the way of Tao.
Whatever is contrary to Tao will not last long.

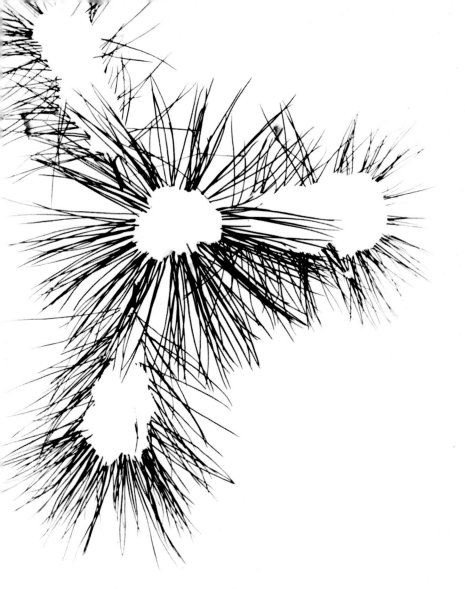

含德之厚比於赤子蜂蠆虺蛇不螫猛獸不據攫鳥不搏骨弱筋柔而握固

未知牝牡之合而全作精之至也終日号而不嗄和之至也

知和曰常知常曰明

益生曰祥心使氣曰强物壯則老謂之不道不道早已

知者不言言者不知塞其兌閉其門

挫其銳解其分和其光同其塵

是謂玄同

故不可得而親不可得而疏不可得而利

不可得而害不可得而貴不可得而賤

故為天下貴

FIFTY-SIX

Those who know do not talk.
Those who talk do not know.

Keep your mouth closed.
Guard your senses.
Temper your sharpness.
Simplify your problems.
Mask your brightness.
Be at one with the dust of the earth.
This is primal union.

He who has achieved this state
Is unconcerned with friends and enemies,
With good and harm, with honor and disgrace.
This therefore is the highest state of man.

以正治國以奇用兵以無事取天下
吾何以知其然哉以此
天下多忌諱而民彌貧民多利器國家滋昏
人多伎巧奇物滋起法令滋彰盜賊多有
故聖人云我無為而民自化我好靜而民自正
我無事而民自富我無欲而民自樸

FIFTY-SEVEN

Rule a nation with justice.
Wage war with surprise moves.
Become master of the universe without striving.
How do I know that this is so?
Because of this!

The more laws and restrictions there are,
The poorer people become.
The sharper men's weapons,
The more trouble in the land.
The more ingenious and clever men are,
The more strange things happen.
The more rules and regulations,
The more thieves and robbers.

Therefore the sage says:
 I take no action and people are reformed.
 I enjoy peace and people become honest.
 I do nothing and people become rich.
 I have no desires and people return to the good and simple life.

其政悶悶其民淳淳其政察察其民缺缺
禍兮福之所倚福兮禍之所伏孰知其極其無正
正復為奇善復為妖人之迷其日固久
是以聖人方而不割廉而不劌直而不肆光而不耀

FIFTY-EIGHT

When the country is ruled with a light hand
The people are simple.
When the country is ruled with severity,
The people are cunning.

Happiness is rooted in misery.
Misery lurks beneath happiness.
Who knows what the future holds?
There is no honesty.
Honesty becomes dishonest.
Goodness becomes witchcraft.
Man's bewitchment lasts for a long time.

Therefore the sage is sharp but not cutting,
Pointed but not piercing,
Straightforward but not unrestrained,
Brilliant but not blinding.

治人事天莫若嗇夫唯嗇是謂早服早服謂之重積德
重積德則無不克無不克則莫知其極莫知其極可以有國
有國之母可以長久是謂深根固柢長生久視之道

FIFTY-NINE

In caring for others and serving heaven,
There is nothing like using restraint.
Restraint begins with giving up one's own ideas.
This depends on Virtue gathered in the past.
If there is a good store of Virtue, then nothing is impossible.
If nothing is impossible, then there are no limits.
If a man knows no limits, then he is fit to be a ruler.
The mother principle of ruling holds good for a long time.
This is called having deep roots and a firm foundation,
The Tao of long life and eternal vision.

治大國若烹小鮮以道莅天下其鬼不神非其鬼不神
其神不傷人非其神不傷人聖人亦不傷人
夫兩不相傷故德交歸焉

SIXTY

Ruling the country is like cooking a small fish.
Approach the universe with Tao,
And evil will have no power.
Not that evil is not powerful,
But its power will not be used to harm others.
Not only will it do no harm to others,
But the sage himself will also be protected.
They do not hurt each other,
And the Virtue in each one refreshes both.

大國者下流天下之交天下之牝

牝常以靜勝牡以靜為下

故大國以下小國則取小國小國以下大國則取大國故或下以取或下而取

大國不過欲兼畜人小國不過欲入事人

夫兩者各得所欲大者宜為下

SIXTY-ONE

A great country is like low land.
It is the meeting ground of the universe,
The mother of the universe.

The female overcomes the male with stillness,
Lying low in stillness.

Therefore if a great country gives way to a smaller country,
It will conquer the smaller country.
And if a small country submits to a great country,
It can conquer the great country.
Therefore those who would conquer must yield,
And those who conquer do so because they yield.

A great nation needs more people;
A small country needs to serve.
Each gets what it wants.
It is fitting for a great nation to yield.

SIXTY-TWO

Tao is the source of the ten thousand things.
It is the treasure of the good man, and the refuge of the bad.
Sweet words can buy honor;
Good deeds can gain respect.
If a man is bad, do not abandon him.
Therefore on the day the emperor is crowned,
Or the three officers of state installed,
Do not send a gift of jade and a team of four horses,
But remain still and offer the Tao.
Why does everyone like the Tao so much at first?
Isn't it because you find what you seek and are forgiven when you sin?
Therefore this is the greatest treasure of the universe.

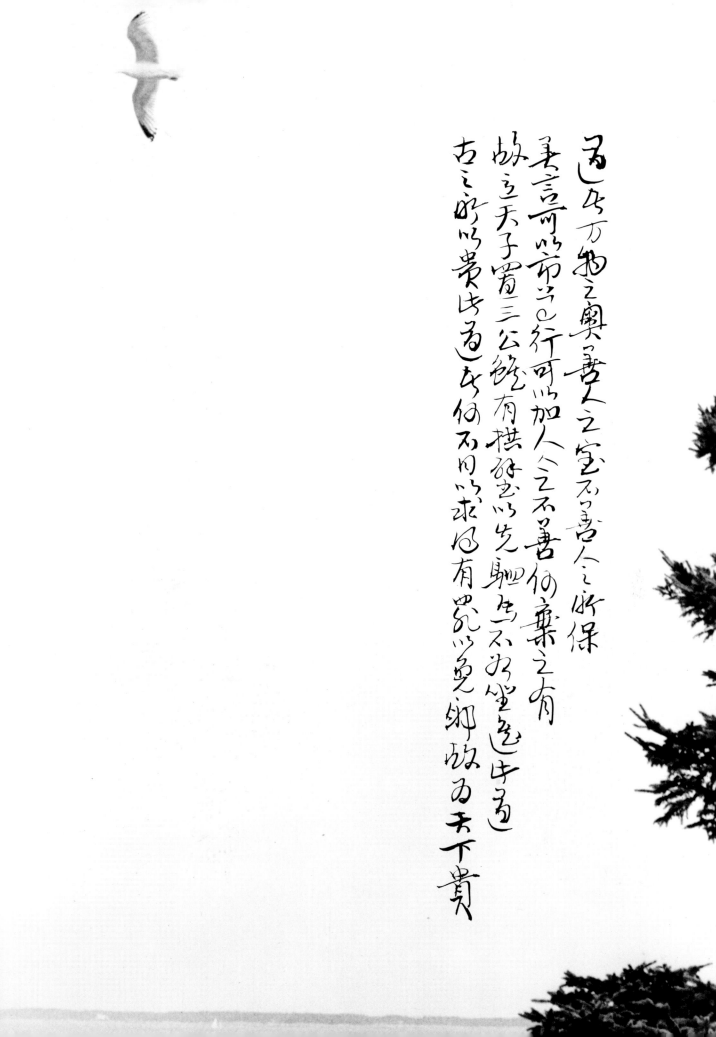

道者万物之奥善人之宝不善人之所保

美言可以市尊行可以加人人之不善何棄之有

故立天子置三公雖有拱璧以先駟馬不如坐進此道

古之所以貴此道者何不曰以求得有罪以免耶故為天下貴

SIXTY-THREE

Practice non-action.
Work without doing.
Taste the tasteless.
Magnify the small, increase the few.
Reward bitterness with care.

See simplicity in the complicated.
Achieve greatness in little things.

In the universe the difficult things are done as if they are easy.
In the universe great acts are made up of small deeds.
The sage does not attempt anything very big,
And thus achieves greatness.

Easy promises make for little trust.
Taking things lightly results in great difficulty.
Because the sage always confronts difficulties,
He never experiences them.

為無為，事無事，味無味。大小多少，報怨以德。圖難於其易，為大於其細。天下難事必作於易，天下大事必作於細。是以聖人終不為大，故能成其大。夫輕諾必寡信，多易必多難。是以聖人猶難之，故終無難矣。

其安易持其未兆易謀其脆易泮其微易散為之於未有治之於未亂

合抱之木生于毫末九層之台起于累土千里之行始于足下

為者敗之執者失之是以聖人無為故無敗無執故無失

此之謂常於幾成而敗之慎終如始則無敗事

是以聖人欲不欲不貴難得之貨學不學復眾人之所過

以輔萬物之自然而不敢為

SIXTY-FOUR

Peace is easily maintained;
Trouble is easily overcome before it starts.
The brittle is easily shattered;
The small is easily scattered.

Deal with it before it happens.
Set things in order before there is confusion.

A tree as great as a man's embrace springs from a small shoot;
A terrace nine stories high begins with a pile of earth;
A journey of a thousand miles starts under one's feet.

He who acts defeats his own purpose;
He who grasps loses.
The sage does not act, and so is not defeated.
He does not grasp and therefore does not lose.

People usually fail when they are on the verge of success.
So give as much care to the end as to the beginning;
Then there will be no failure.

Therefore the sage seeks freedom from desire.
He does not collect precious things.
He learns not to hold on to ideas.
He brings men back to what they have lost.
He helps the ten thousand things find their own nature,
But refrains from action.

SIXTY-FIVE

In the beginning those who knew the Tao did not try to enlighten others,
But kept them in the dark.
Why is it so hard to rule?
Because people are so clever.
Rulers who try to use cleverness
Cheat the country.
Those who rule without cleverness
Are a blessing to the land.
These are the two alternatives.
Understanding these is Primal Virtue.
Primal Virtue is deep and far.
It leads all things back
Toward the great oneness.

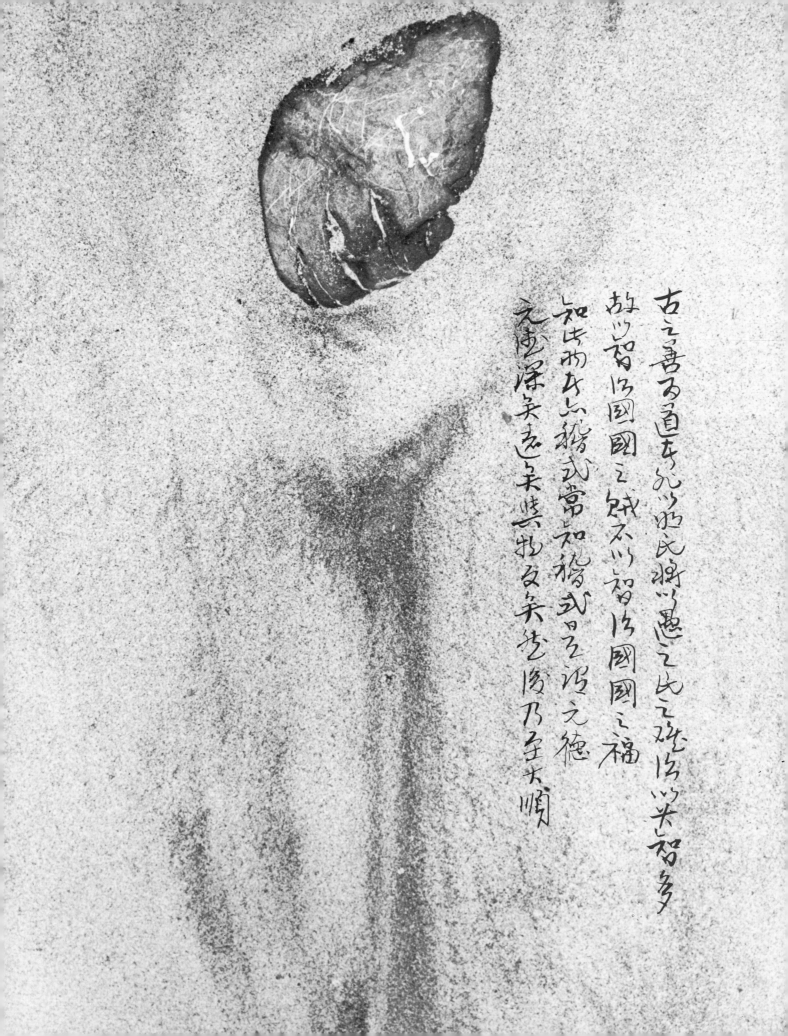

古之善為道者非以明民將以愚之民之難治以其智多
故以智治國國之賊不以智治國國之福
知此兩者亦稽式常知稽式是謂玄德
玄德深矣遠矣與物反矣然後乃至大順

江海所以能為百谷王者以其善下之故能為百谷王

是以欲上民必以言下之欲先民必以身後之

是以聖人處上而民不重處前而民不害

是以天下樂推而不厭以其不爭故天下莫能與之爭

SIXTY-SIX

Why is the sea king of a hundred streams?
Because it lies below them.
Therefore it is the king of a hundred streams.

If the sage would guide the people, he must serve with humility.
If he would lead them, he must follow behind.
In this way when the sage rules, the people will not feel oppressed;
When he stands before them, they will not be harmed.
The whole world will support him and will not tire of him.

Because he does not compete,
He does not meet competition.

SIXTY-SEVEN

Everyone under heaven says that my Tao is great and beyond compare.
Because it is great, it seems different.
If it were not different, it would have vanished long ago.

I have three treasures which I hold and keep.
The first is mercy; the second is economy;
The third is daring not to be ahead of others.
From mercy comes courage; from economy comes generosity;
From humility comes leadership.

Nowadays men shun mercy, but try to be brave;
They abandon economy, but try to be generous;
They do not believe in humility, but always try to be first.
This is certain death.

Mercy brings victory in battle and strength in defense.
It is the means by which heaven saves and guards.

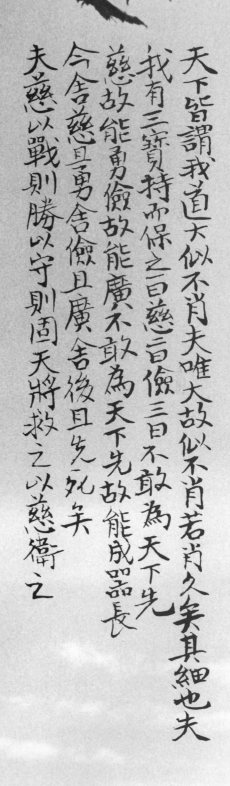

天下皆謂我道大似不肖夫唯大故似不肖若肖久矣其細也夫
我有三寶持而保之一曰慈二曰儉三曰不敢為天下先
慈故能勇儉故能廣不敢為天下先故能成器長
今舍慈且勇舍儉且廣舍後且先死矣
夫慈以戰則勝以守則固天將救之以慈衛之

善為士者不武、善戰者不怒、善勝敵者不與、善用人者為之下、是謂不爭之德、是謂用人之力、是謂配天古之極

SIXTY-EIGHT

A good soldier is not violent.
A good fighter is not angry.
A good winner is not vengeful.
A good employer is humble.
This is known as the Virtue of not striving.
This is known as ability to deal with people.
This since ancient times has been known
    as the ultimate unity with heaven.

用兵有言吾不敢為主而為客不敢進寸而退尺
是謂行無行攘無臂扔無敵執無兵
禍莫大於輕敵輕敵幾喪吾寶故抗兵相加哀者勝矣

SIXTY-NINE

There is a saying among soldiers:
 I dare not make the first move but would rather play the guest;
 I dare not advance an inch but would rather withdraw a foot.

This is called marching without appearing to move,
Rolling up your sleeves without showing your arm,
Capturing the enemy without attacking,
Being armed without weapons.

There is no greater catastrophe than underestimating the enemy.
By underestimating the enemy, I almost lose what I value.

Therefore when the battle is joined,
The underdog will win.

SEVENTY

My words are easy to understand and easy to perform,
Yet no man under heaven knows them or practices them.

My words have ancient beginnings.
My actions are disciplined.
Because men do not understand, they have no knowledge of me.

Those that know me are few;
Those that abuse me are honored.
Therefore the sage wears rough clothing and holds the jewel in his heart.

吾言甚易知甚易行天下莫能知莫能行
言有宗事有君夫唯無知是以不我知
知我者希則我者貴是以聖人被褐懷玉

SEVENTY-ONE

Knowing ignorance is strength.
Ignoring knowledge is sickness.

If one is sick of sickness, then one is not sick.
The sage is not sick because he is sick of sickness.
Therefore he is not sick.

知不知上不知知病夫唯病病是以不病聖人不病以其病病是以不病

民不畏威則大威至
無狎其所居無厭其所生夫唯不厭是以不厭
是以聖人自知不自見自愛不自貴故去彼取此

SEVENTY-TWO

When men lack a sense of awe, there will be disaster.

Do not intrude in their homes.
Do not harass them at work.
If you do not interfere, they will not weary of you.

Therefore the sage knows himself but makes no show,
Has self-respect but is not arrogant.
He lets go of that and chooses this.

SEVENTY-THREE

A brave and passionate man will kill or be killed.
A brave and calm man will always preserve life.
Of these two which is good and which is harmful?
Some things are not favored by heaven. Who knows why?
Even the sage is unsure of this.

The Tao of heaven does not strive, and yet it overcomes.
It does not speak, and yet is answered.
It does not ask, yet is supplied with all its needs.
It seems at ease, and yet it follows a plan.

Heaven's net casts wide.
Though its meshes are coarse, nothing slips through.

勇於敢則殺勇於不敢則活此兩者或利或害
天之所惡孰知其故是以聖人猶難之
天之道不爭而善勝不言而善應不召而自來
繟然而善謀天網恢恢疏而不失

民不畏死奈何以死懼之
若使民常畏死而為奇者吾得執而殺之孰敢
常有司殺者殺夫代司殺者殺是謂代大匠斲
夫代大匠斲者希有不傷其手矣

SEVENTY-FOUR

If men are not afraid to die,
It is of no avail to threaten them with death.

If men live in constant fear of dying,
And if breaking the law means that a man will be killed,
Who will dare to break the law?

There is always an official executioner.
If you try to take his place,
It is like trying to be a master carpenter and cutting wood.
If you try to cut wood like a master carpenter,
    you will only hurt your hand.

民之饑以其上食稅之多是以饑民之難治以其上之有為是以難治民之輕死以其上求生之厚是以輕死夫唯無以生為者是賢於貴生

SEVENTY-FIVE

Why are the people starving?
Because the rulers eat up the money in taxes.
Therefore the people are starving.

Why are the people rebellious?
Because the rulers interfere too much.
Therefore they are rebellious.

Why do the people think so little of death?
Because the rulers demand too much of life.
Therefore the people take death lightly.

Having little to live on, one knows better than to value life too much.

人之生也柔弱其死也堅強萬物草木之生也柔脆其死也枯槁故堅強者死之徒柔弱者生之徒是以兵強則不勝木強則兵強大處下柔弱處上

SEVENTY-SIX

A man is born gentle and weak.
At his death he is hard and stiff.
Green plants are tender and filled with sap.
At their death they are withered and dry.

Therefore the stiff and unbending is the disciple of death.
The gentle and yielding is the disciple of life.

Thus an army without flexibility never wins a battle.
A tree that is unbending is easily broken.

The hard and strong will fall.
The soft and weak will overcome.

SEVENTY-SEVEN

The Tao of heaven is like the bending of a bow.
The high is lowered, and the low is raised.
If the string is too long, it is shortened;
If there is not enough, it is made longer.

The Tao of heaven is to take from those who have too much
    and give to those who do not have enough.
Man's way is different.
He takes from those who do not have enough
    to give to those who already have too much.
What man has more than enough and gives it to the world?
Only the man of Tao.

Therefore the sage works without recognition.
He achieves what has to be done without dwelling on it.
He does not try to show his knowledge.

天之道其猶張弓與 高者抑之下者舉之

有餘者損之不足者補之

天之道損有餘而補不足人之道則不然損不足以奉有餘

孰能有餘以奉天下唯有道者

是以聖人為而不恃功成而不處其不欲見賢

天下莫柔弱於水而攻堅強者莫之能勝以其無以易之

弱之勝強柔之勝剛天下莫不知莫能行

是以聖人云受國之垢是謂社稷主受國不祥

是為天下王正言若反

SEVENTY-EIGHT

Under heaven nothing is more soft and yielding than water.
Yet for attacking the solid and strong, nothing is better;
It has no equal.
The weak can overcome the strong;
The supple can overcome the stiff.
Under heaven everyone knows this,
Yet no one puts it into practice.
Therefore the sage says:
    He who takes upon himself the humiliation of the people
        is fit to rule them.
    He who takes upon himself the country's disasters deserves
        to be king of the universe.
The truth often sounds paradoxical.

和大怨必有餘怨安可以為善是以聖人執左契
而不責於人有德司契無德司徹
天道無親常與善人

SEVENTY-NINE

After a bitter quarrel, some resentment must remain.
What can one do about it?
Therefore the sage keeps his half of the bargain
But does not exact his due.
A man of Virtue performs his part,
But a man without Virtue requires others to fulfill their obligations.
The Tao of heaven is impartial.
It stays with good men all the time.

小國寡民使有什伯之器而不用

使民重死而不遠徙雖有舟輿無所乘之

雖有甲兵無所陳之使人復結繩而用之

甘其食美其服安其居乐其俗

鄰國相望鷄犬之声相聞

民至老死不相往来

EIGHTY

A small country has fewer people.
Though there are machines that can work ten to a hundred times faster
    than man, they are not needed.
The people take death seriously and do not travel far.
Though they have boats and carriages, no one uses them.
Though they have armor and weapons, no one displays them.
Men return to the knotting of rope in place of writing.
Their food is plain and good, their clothes fine but simple,
    their homes secure;
They are happy in their ways.
Though they live within sight of their neighbors,
And crowing cocks and barking dogs are heard across the way,
Yet they leave each other in peace while they grow old and die.

信言不美美言不信善者不辯辯者不善知者不博博者不知

聖人不積既以為人己愈有既以與人己愈多

天之道利而不害聖人之道為而不爭

EIGHTY-ONE

Truthful words are not beautiful.
Beautiful words are not truthful.
Good men do not argue.
Those who argue are not good.
Those who know are not learned.
The learned do not know.

The sage never tries to store things up.
The more he does for others, the more he has.
The more he gives to others, the greater his abundance.
The Tao of heaven is pointed but does no harm.
The Tao of the sage is work without effort.

The following is an excerpt from unpublished autobiographical writings by Gia-fu Feng, printed here with only minimal editing. Living from 1919 to 1985, he spent half his life in China and half in the USA. While his life spanned two very different cultures and times of great change and turmoil, it was rooted in the ancient Chinese culture of which the Tao Te Ching *is a part.*

During the summertime when we were out of school, we often spent our two hot months in our summer home in the suburbs of Shanghai. There were nine of us kids with a troop of servants, chauffeurs, gardeners, bodyguards, and an old tutor, Master Shuan, who was a scholar of the old school with a title of Hang-Ting from the Ching Dynasty (comparable to a Rhodes Scholar in the West).

He was very old-fashioned and a little out of touch with rapidly Westernizing Shanghai mores. He would sometimes take a nap in the classroom during the hot summer noon. We would make fun of him by hiding his glasses, etc., but Chao-shu (my younger brother) was always his best friend. Chao-shu was the most congenial soul in our household.

In the morning at 9 A.M. we had a British woman, a certain Miss Gawler (I never knew her first name because it was improper to call her by her first name), who was the sister of the British Commissioner of the Shanghai Customs, to teach us English conversation for two hours. We were always unprepared for her arrival because Master Shuan gave us so much homework to do, plus we liked to stay up late at night.

First thing in the morning, we had to do two sheets of calligraphy. These had to be done before even brushing our teeth. With our eyes barely open, we started to grind our ink blocks against our ink stones. Each one of us had a particular piece of stone engravings to copy, the originals being done by the great calligraphers of the Tang, Soong, and Ming Dynasties. Master Shuan would look over our calligraphy very carefully each day. For the good ones, he would circle at the upper right hand corner with red ink. For the bad ones, he would put a diagonal stroke across them from the upper left hand to the lower right hand corner. We would compare with each other the number of circles and diagonal strokes respectively to know our scores, high or low.

After our practice of calligraphy, we had to chant a specific section of the Chinese classics for the day in order to recite it in front of Master Shuan later. There was so much to be done in the mornings that sometimes we missed breakfast. We were terribly rushed because we had to dress properly to confront the proper British lady. Chao-shu was always the first one who was ready. He would stand at the door waiting for the lady to arrive and would entertain her with a cup of tea while the rest of us were running down the stairway to be in our seats before the class was to begin. My senior-high-school years were perhaps the best learning years of my entire life. I really got to learn when I was fifteen. I was tutored by the finest classical scholars available.

I even studied Chinese music. I specialized in *er-wu*, which was a two-stringed fiddle with a bow made of horse tail. It sat on the lap vertically, unlike the violin that was put under the chin horizontally. The Chinese music teacher would come in the late afternoon after our main course of study was over. By that time we were fed up with the classic verses, chanting and memorizing. It was time for a break. The Chinese music notes were five tones, which were represented by five calligraphic characters. The old teacher would chant the sounds aloud while tapping out the beats either by slapping his knees, waving his hand, or nodding his head.

In 1937, when I was eighteen, the Japanese invaded northern China proper, which triggered the Sino-Japanese war and eventually World War II. The golden age of Chinese classical learning was over.

—Gia-fu Feng

Gia-fu playing an er-wu he purchased in San Francisco's Chinatown in 1973

Gia-fu Feng and I shared the same birthplace in Shanghai, China, and a similar heritage of early intensive classical Chinese studies. When we first discovered each other in America in the early 1970s, we delighted in recounting childhood memories of learning *I Ching* and *Tao Te Ching* and practicing Tai Ji and brush calligraphy. And we realized we were privileged to share our knowledge of these experiences with so many people in the West.

The fundamental difference between Eastern and Western views is that the West focuses on individualism, where personal ego looms in the center. In the East, especially in the Chinese Taoist tradition, the most important learning is a sense of belonging to a larger whole. It opens a wider universal vista in which the personal ego can connect and expand. While the West tries to forge ahead, the East values retreat, when necessary to create space for an extended perspective.

In the West we depend on reason and logic. Concretized, factual, and proven things become our security. We crave absolute answers, leaving little room for creative and spiritual inquiry, for "maybe" and "perhaps," and for the unknown. Whereas, it has been part of Eastern thinking to accept and celebrate the mystery that we may never understand. But, all too often, the West gallops with giant heedless strides to break barriers, while the East stagnates in outdated traditions.

As industrialized nations rely on technology, information, and accumulated knowledge, which secure an array of material conveniences, they tend to overlook the human thirst for wisdom in the deeper meaning of life. Conversely, the East is intuitively in tune with nature and cosmic consciousness, yet feels its own kind of longing for a well defined mechanistic model of reality, and for the excitement of free and creative expression. The ideal integration is to embrace this paradox of East and West, with open hearts and minds, to create a balanced global synthesis.

Both Gia-fu and I were lucky to have had a traditional upbringing, and to have been classically disciplined and cultivated for life in China. And we were fortunate to be young and open-minded, resilient and flexible, when we were transplanted to a different culture. We were able to experience the "American dream" while maintaining our own culture. He studied business; I became an architect and dancer. We learned to become teachers, combining our bi-cultural riches to impart the most innovative and joyous aspects of this synthesis. We proved that the TAO transcends being merely Chinese.

It is with great joy and humility I participate in this anniversary edition of *Tao Te Ching*, to honor Gia-fu and Jane, to bow to Lao Tsu, and to celebrate the Eternal TAO.

—Chungliang Al Huang

Chungliang Al Huang is an internationally respected Tai Ji master and authority on East/West cultural synthesis. He is the author of the classic Embrace Tiger, Return to Mountain *and of* Quantum Soup; *co-author with Alan Watts of* Tao: The Watercourse Way *and with Jerry Lynch of* Thinking Body, Dancing Mind *and* Mentoring: The Tao of Giving and Receiving Wisdom.

The following is an excerpt from the article "What Constitutes a 'Necessary' Book" by Toinette Lippe, originally published in The Collegiate Review, *Fall 1985.*

The *Tao Te Ching* was one of the very first books I worked on while an editor at Alfred A. Knopf. I was sitting quietly in my office one day when the receptionist called to say that there were two people outside with a manuscript. Their names were Gia-fu Feng and Jane English and they wished to see me. Now one thing you learn very early on if you are an editor: Try to read something of an author's work *before* you sit down and talk to him. Otherwise there is very little to discuss, since the author has read what he has written and you have not. In this case, not only had I not read anything by these people, I didn't even know who they were. But something stopped me saying, "Tell them to leave the manuscript. I'm busy now. I'll be in touch when I've read it." I found myself walking out to the receptionist and returning to my office with a small Ho Chi Minh–like figure, complete with wispy beard, and his tall, strong American companion. I sat them down and asked them what brought them there.

They told me that Macmillan, whose offices were across the street, had published Gia-fu Feng's first book *Tai Chi and I Ching* but that his editor had left and the young man who had read the new manuscript and liked it was also leaving at the end of the week, so there was no one at Macmillan with any enthusiasm for the book. The young man recommended that the manuscript be shown to me. I was very taken aback. I had met this young man a couple of times but did not think that he knew that I practiced the ancient Chinese exercise of tai chi chuan. When I mentioned this to them, they expressed surprise and delight. The man at Macmillan had not known about this at all but had simply felt that I might be open to the possibility of publishing their new book, which was a translation of the *Tao Te Ching*. He was right. I sat and turned the pages in wonder. Each verse was accompanied by Chinese calligraphy and an exquisite photograph. I persuaded them to leave the manuscript with me so I could show it to the editor-in-chief.

When I took it to him, he saw immediately that the photos were magnificent but he also pointed out that I knew nothing about publishing photographic books. I agreed with him but said that I had a hunch about this book. He believed me, for some curious reason, and I started work immediately. As I studied the translation, I realized that it had quite a way to go before it would measure up to Jane English's photographs. I consulted other translations and was amazed to discover that Lao Tsu's *Tao Te Ching* had been translated into English more times than any other work except the Bible. Still, the more of these I read, the more I realized how inaccessible many of them were. I don't read Chinese and so I could not compare anything with the original. Instead, I picked about a dozen translations ranging from Arthur Waley's historically accurate version to Witter Bynner's lyrical poem, which seemed to take liberties with the text while perfectly expressing the spirit.

I would read how each of these twelve had translated a particular line and then go back to Gia-fu's translation to see what he thought the line meant. Then I would find a way to express his understanding in a simple, rhythmical natural way and in words that had not been used by other translators. It was the opposite of plagiarism! Finally, I would read each page to a young Mexican friend and if it did not read well aloud or if she looked puzzled, I would adjust the words or the cadence until the meaning was clearly delivered. I then sent the new text to Gia-fu, who would approve (or disapprove occasionally) of what I had done. I have the suspicion that he thought that this was the normal editorial process; which it is not.

Gia-fu Feng and Jane English in 1971
Photograph from the jacket of
the 1972 hardcover edition of Tao Te Ching

At last, when the book was nearly ready for publication, came the moment every editor dreads—the writing of jacket copy—when the essence of the whole book has to be expressed in a few sentences so that anyone picking up the book will know by perusing the cover what is to be found within. How could I possibly reduce this sixth-century-B.C. classic to a single paragraph? Weeks had gone by and finally I had only twenty minutes left. I sat down before the typewriter and my mind went blank. I waited a little while and then began to type. I'm still amazed at what appeared on the page, for while I might now change quite a lot of the translation, I wouldn't alter a word of what appears on the outside of the book:

Accept what is in front of you without wanting the situation to be other than it is. Study the natural order of things and work with it rather than against it, for to try to change what is only sets up resistance . . . . We serve whatever or whoever stands before us, without any thought for ourselves. Te—which may be translated as "virtue" or "strength"—lies always in Tao, or "natural law." In other words: Simply be.

The rest is history (recent history). The book was very well received and all kinds of people would recommend it to me as something I might like or tell me how it was the one book they took to a cabin in the mountains. Well over half a million copies have been sold in this country alone and the book continues to sell several hundred copies a week. Perhaps the final word came from *Time* magazine, where it was described as "the *Tao Te Ching* gussied up with photographs." As I said to the reviewer, who eventually came to work, as I do, at Knopf, "It's true, but until it was gussied up with photographs, the *Tao Te Ching* had been around for 2,500 years and *Time* magazine hadn't bothered to review it."

Toinette Lippe is now editorial director of Bell Tower.

ABOUT THE TRANSLATORS

Gia-fu Feng was born in Shanghai in 1919, was educated in China, and came to the United States in 1947 to study comparative religion. He held a BA from Peking University and an MA from the University of Pennsylvania. He taught at Esalen Institute in Big Sur, California, and directed Stillpoint Foundation, a Taoist community in Colorado. Gia-fu Feng died in 1985.

Jane English, whose photographs form an integral part of this book, holds a BA from Mount Holyoke College and received her doctorate from the University of Wisconsin in experimental high energy particle physics. In 1985, she founded her own publishing business, Earth Heart. Her books and calendars include *Different Doorway: Adventures of a Caesarean Born, Mount Shasta: Where Heaven and Earth Meet* (with Jenny Coyle) and the yearly *Tao Te Ching Calendar*. She was born in Boston, Massachusetts, in 1942.

Chuang Tsu/*Inner Chapters* (1974), a companion volume to Lao Tsu/*Tao Te Ching*, is a direct outcome of the successful collaboration between Gia-fu Feng and Jane English on the *Tao Te Ching*.

RESOURCES

Since this book was first published numerous books on Taoism and related subjects have been published, and several Taoist organizations have been created here in the United States. The following list gives a few of these.

Living Tao Foundation
Lan Ting Institute
PO Box 846, Urbana, IL 61803
Tel/Fax: 217-337-6113

Living Tao Foundation is a non-profit global membership network founded in 1976 by Chungliang Al Huang. It offers seminars and training programs internationally in Taoist principles applicable to successful modern living. The focus is on Taoist classics, Tai Ji movement and its related disciplines as mirror reflections of our lifelong learning process.

The foundation also offers video and audio tapes, books and art prints/posters and calligraphic art shirts; and periodically, specially designed cross-cultural exchange programs in China's sacred mountains and in the West.

The Abode of the Eternal Tao
1991 Garfield, Eugene, OR 97405
Tel: 541-345-8854
Publisher of:

The Empty Vessel—a quarterly journal of contemporary Taoism.

A Gathering of Cranes: Bringing the Tao to the West—a collection of interviews with many well-known Taoist teachers.

Genesee Valley Daoist Hermitage
1010 Genesee-Troy Rd., Genesee, ID 83832
Tel. 208-285-0123

An environment for self-cultivation involving sustainable farming practices, qigong practice, Chang Ming nutrition, meditation, and Daoist lifestyle practices. Off-site teaching of life skills which support Daoist philosophy and sustain health. Travel/study programs in China.

Earth Heart
PO Box 7, Mount Shasta, CA 96067
Tel: 530-926-2751, Fax 530-926-5537
Order phone: 530-926-5076
www.eheart.com

Publisher of other books and calendars illustrated with photographs by Jane English

Amber Lotus
PO Box 31538, San Francisco, CA 94131
Tel: 415-864-7388, Fax 415-864-7399
Order phone: 800-326-2375
www.amberlotus.com
Publisher of:

Tao Te Ching Calendar—Annual wall calendar using twelve chapters from this book.

Chuang Tsu: Inner Chapters—New edition of the companion volume to this book, first published in 1974. New introduction by Chungliang Al Huang.

Notecards of photographs by Jane English

Vintage Books
299 Park Avenue, New York, NY 10171
Tel. 800-793-2665
Publisher of:

Tao Te Ching—Pocket edition of this translation of *Tao Te Ching*, with introduction and notes by Jacob Needleman, but without photographs and calligraphy.

Audio Literature
370 West San Bruno Avenue, San Bruno, CA 94066
Tel: 800-383-0174
Publisher of:

Tao Te Ching—Two cassette tapes containing Jacob Needleman's unabridged reading of the text of this book and his commentary.

Chuang Tsu: Inner Chapters—Two cassette tapes of Chungliang Al Huang's unabridged reading of the text, with some also read in Chinese, plus his flute music.

A Note on the Variation of Chinese Spellings:

In recent years, the People's Republic of China replaced the Wade-Giles system of phonetics with the *pinyin* system, changing *Tao* to *Dao* and *T'ai Chi* to *Tai Ji* in order to rectify mispronunciations of words like *Peking*, now spelled *Beijing*. For consistency and to match the still persistent Wade-Giles system in academic studies, most people still prefer Tao to Dao. But Tai Ji is commonly used to distinguish Ji from Chi, which is a separate symbol in Chinese.